Copyright © 2020 by V(

RND

All rights reserved. No part of this publication may be reproduced, distributed, or transmitted in any form or by any means, including photocopying, recording, or other electronic or mechanical methods, without the prior written permission of the publisher, except in the case of brief quotations embodied in critical reviews and certain other noncommercial uses permitted by copyright law

Table of Contents

Table of Contents 2

Introduction 4

List of Vegetarian Mexican Recipes 6

    Cauliflower Tacos 6

    Vegan Nachos 10

    Refried Bean Tacos 13

    Best Pico de Gallo 17

    Mexican Pizza 19

    Loaded Quinoa Tacos 24

    Best Jackfruit Tacos 30

    Quinoa Vegetarian Enchiladas 35

    Black Bean Burrito 42

Vegan Fajitas 46

Vegetarian Tortilla Soup 51

Crispy Avocado Tacos 56

Easy Mexican Salad 59

Mexican Coleslaw 63

Quinoa Taco Meat 66

Cream of Corn Soup 69

Vegan Mexican Lasagna 74

Easy Calabacitas 79

One Skillet Mexican Quinoa Dinner 84

Easy Mexican Street Corn (Elotes) 86

Introduction

Traditional Mexican food is inherently plant-based, which makes the cuisine particularly suited for vegetarian and vegan eaters. Corn, avocado, tomatoes, beans, and rice are all core ingredients in most Mexican dishes. Besides being nutrient-rich, these ingredients are also sustainable and inexpensive, a triple win. All of this is to say: cooking up plant-based, Mexican food is easier than you think. Plus, depending on your interpretation of a plant-based diet (from eating a little meat and cheese to eating no animal products at all), there are tons of tasty dishes that will fit the bill.

However, it can be hard to reimagine your favorite Mexican dishes sans meat without just defaulting to another meal of rice and beans. To give you some cooking inspiration, check out these 20 delicious vegetarian Mexican recipes. Whether you're craving tacos, quesadillas, enchiladas, or another classic dish, you're sure to find your new favorite go-to recipe here.

List of Vegetarian Mexican Recipes

Cauliflower Tacos

These cauliflower tacos with breaded cauliflower, refried beans and silky yum yum sauce are all about one thing, what a big flavor.

Ingredients

- 1 recipe Crispy Breaded Cauliflower
- 15-ounce can vegetarian refried beans (or Easy Refried Black Beans or Homemade Refried Beans)

- 1/2 teaspoon cumin
- 2 cups red cabbage, shredded
- 2 limes (1 for the cabbage & 1 to serve)
- 3 tablespoons Yum Yum Sauce or Spicy Chipotle Sauce
- 8 corn tortillas
- Fresh cilantro, for garnish

Instructions

1. Make the Crispy Breaded Cauliflower (about 40 minutes total)
2. If using purchased refried beans, taste and if needed, mix with 1/2 teaspoon cumin and/or a pinch or two kosher salt.

3. Thinly slice the cabbage, enough for 2 cups. Mix it with 2 tablespoons lime juice and a pinch or two of salt.
4. Allow it to stand at room temperature until serving.
5. Make the Yum Yum Sauce or Spicy Chipotle Sauce.
6. Warm the tortillas, or char them by placing them on grates above an open gas flame on medium heat for a few seconds per side, flipping with tongs, until they are slightly blackened and warm.
7. Chop the cilantro for a garnish.

8. To serve, place refried beans in a tortilla, top with cabbage, breaded cauliflower, Yum Yum sauce, and cilantro.

9. Serve with lime wedges to spritz prior to serving.

Note: If you have leftover cauliflower, you can reheat them in a 350F oven for 10 minutes, flipping once.)

Vegan Nachos

These loaded vegan nachos are the best because they're piled high with smoky, meaty lentils, crunchy veggies, and topped with our vegan nacho cheese. To keep them healthy, look for organic corn chips with minimal ingredients (ideally corn, oil, and salt).

Ingredients

- 2 cups Smoky Instant Pot Lentils or Lentil Taco Filling, or 1 recipe Refried Black Beans or Refried Bean Dip (using canned refried beans)
- 1/4 cup Vegan Nacho Cheese

- 1 small tomato or Best Salsa Recipe
- 1/4 red onion
- 1 to 2 green onions
- 4 cups organic corn chips
- Fresh cilantro, for garnish
- Hot sauce, for garnish
- **Optional:** Pickled jalapenos, Pickled onions, or Pickled radishes

Instructions

1. Make the Smoky Instant Pot Lentils and Rice or Lentil Taco Filling. Before serving, make sure the lentils are warm (reheat them if made in advance).

2. Make the Vegan Nacho Cheese.

3. Seed and dice the tomato. Mince the red onion. Thinly slice the green onions. Chop the cilantro. (or, make Salsa Fresca for topping.)

4. To serve, place the chips on a plate. Top with lentils, tomato, red onion, green onion, Vegan Nacho Cheese, cilantro, and hot sauce.

Refried Bean Tacos

These refried bean tacos are a simple, healthy plant based dinner idea. They're full of flavor and served with a smoky chipotle cream.

Ingredients

For the refried bean tacos

- 1 recipe Easy Refried Black Beans or Homemade Refried Beans (or 1 1/2 cups Instant Pot Refried Beans)
- 2 cups shredded green cabbage
- 1/2 red bell pepper
- 1/2 yellow bell pepper

- 2 tablespoons fresh lime juice (1 lime)
- 1/4 teaspoon kosher salt
- Fresh ground black pepper
- 8 One Degree Organics sprouted corn tortillas
- 1 large handful cilantro leaves

For the chipotle cream

- 1 recipe Vegan Sour Cream or Cashew Cream (or substitute 1 cup sour cream for non-vegan option)
- 1 tablespoon adobo sauce (from 1 can chipotle peppers in adobo sauce)

Instructions

1. Start soaking the cashews for the chipotle cream (1 hour in advance is best; you can do 30 minutes if you have a high speed blender. Or you can soak the night before and refrigerate until making the cream).
2. Make the Supremely Simple Black Beans.
3. Meanwhile, thinly slice the cabbage. Thinly slice the peppers (cut off the rounded edges of the peppers so that the peppers are straight). Juice the lime.
4. Just before serving, mix together the cabbage, peppers, lime juice, kosher salt and several grinds of black pepper in a large bowl.

5. After the cashews have soaked, make the cashew cream using these instructions, adding in the adobo sauce with the rest of the ingredients to make chipotle cream.
6. Warm the tortillas or char them by placing them on grates above an open gas flame on medium heat for a few seconds per side, flipping with tongs, until they are slightly blackened and warm.
7. To serve, place refried beans in a tortilla, top with cabbage and pepper slaw, chipotle cream, and some torn cilantro leaves.

Best Pico de Gallo

This best pico de gallo recipe is always a home run. Just 6 ingredients, it's the ideal dip for tortilla chips and topping for fish or tacos.

Ingredients

- 1 1/2 pounds ripe red tomatoes (about 4 medium), enough for 2 cups finely diced
- 1/2 cup minced white onion (about 1/4 large onion)
- 1 to 2 jalapeño peppers, seeds removed (depending on your spice tolerance)
- 1/4 cup packed finely chopped cilantro
- 1/4 teaspoon cumin

- 2 tablespoons lime juice
- 1/2 teaspoon kosher salt

Instructions

1. Dice the tomatoes, removing the core and seeds.
2. Finely chop the onion. Remove the seeds from the jalapeño peppers and finely chop them. Finely chop the cilantro.
3. Mix the tomatoes, onion, jalapeño peppers, cilantro, cumin, lime juice, and kosher salt in a bowl.
4. Serve immediately. You can store a few days refrigerated as well. The pico de gallo will

accumulate water as it sits; drain as necessary.

Mexican Pizza

This Mexican pizza recipe features creamy refried beans, spicy jalapeño, and sweet corn. The perfect dish for when you can't decide what to make!

Ingredients

- 2 balls Best Pizza Dough (or Food Processor Dough or Thin Crust Dough)
- 1 cup canned refried black beans (or Refried Black Beans, Refried Pinto Beans, or Instant Pot Refried Beans
- 1/2 teaspoon cumin
- 1/4 teaspoon paprika
- 1/4 teaspoon cayenne
- 1 small green onion
- 1 tomato
- 1 jalapeño pepper (or more to taste)
- 2 handfuls frozen corn
- Mexican cheese blend (or a mix of Monterrey jack and cheddar)

- Kosher salt

- Fresh cilantro

- Sour cream or Mexican Crema, to serve **(optional)**

- Pickled onions, to serve **(optional)**

Instructions

1. Prepare the dough using the Best Pizza Dough Recipe. Follow the preparation instructions in the dough recipe if prepared in advance.

2. Place a pizza stone in the oven and preheat to 500°F. or preheat your pizza oven.

3. In a medium bowl, mix the refried black beans with a bit of water to thin the consistency so that it is easily spreadable.

4. Mix with 1/2 teaspoon cumin, 1/4 teaspoon paprika, and 1/4 teaspoon cayenne.

5. Seed and dice the tomato. Thinly slice the green onion.

6. Seed and dice the jalapeño or if you prefer, thinly slice it. Chop the cilantro.

7. When the oven is ready, dust a pizza peel with cornmeal or semolina flour. (If you don't have a pizza peel, you can use a rimless baking sheet or the back of a rimmed baking sheet.

8. Stretch the dough into a circle then gently place the dough onto the pizza peel.

9. Quickly assemble the pizza. Spread the bean mixture in a thin layer over the dough.

10. Sprinkle on as much cheese as you like, and add the red onion, tomato, jalapeño, corn, and cilantro.

11. Sprinkle with kosher salt (very important – this really brings out the flavors!).

12. Transfer the pizza to the pizza stone using the pizza peel, and bake until the cheese and crust are nicely browned, about 5 to 7 minutes.

13. **Note:** Repeat Steps 4 through 6 for the second pizza (if your stone isn't big enough for two!).
14. Chop the cilantro and add it as a garnish.
15. Add sour cream and pickled onions, if desired.

Loaded Quinoa Tacos

These loaded quinoa tacos are a delicious vegetarian taco recipe, featuring quinoa taco filling, bell pepper slaw, spicy sour cream, and feta.

Ingredients

- 1 cup Simply Nature Organic Quinoa
- 2 cups Simply Nature Organic Vegetable Broth
- 3 tablespoons Simply Nature Organic Coconut Oil
- 1 tablespoon each: cumin and paprika
- 1 teaspoon each: garlic powder, onion powder, and oregano
- 1/2 teaspoon kosher salt, divided
- 2 green onions
- 1 lime
- 1 bell peppers
- 4 cups Simply Nature Organic Spring Mix
- Salsa, store bought or Salsa Fresca

- Sour cream, spicy mayo, or cashew cream
- Feta cheese crumbles (omit for vegan)
- Pickled red onions, pickled radishes or pickled jalapenos (optional, made in advance)
- 10 to 12 corn tortillas

Instructions

1. **Cook the quinoa:** In a dry pan over medium heat, add the dry quinoa and toast it over medium heat, stirring frequently.
2. After a few minutes you'll start to hear a popping sound; continue stirring until the

quinoa just starts to brown and smell toasty, about 3 to 4 minutes total.

3. Immediately transfer the quinoa to a fine mesh strainer and rinse it in the sink.
4. Return it to the pot and add the vegetable broth and 1/4 teaspoon kosher salt. Bring it to a boil, then reduce the heat to low.
5. Cover the pot and simmer where the broth is just bubbling for about 15 to 20 minutes, until the broth has been completely absorbed. (Check by pulling back the quinoa with a fork to see if broth remains.)
6. Turn off the heat and let sit with the lid on to steam for 5 minutes, then fluff the quinoa with a fork.

7. **Prepare the toppings:** While the quinoa cooks, make a quick bell pepper slaw: Thinly slice the peppers, then cut them in half.

8. Place them in a bowl and mix with 1 tablespoon lime juice and a few pinches kosher salt, and allow to stand until serving.

   Note: If serving with spicy sour cream, stir in few shakes hot sauce to taste (or do the same with hummus for a vegan option).

9. **Finish the quinoa taco filling:** When quinoa is done, melt the coconut oil in large nonstick pan over medium heat.

10. Add cooked quinoa and stir to combine. Add the cumin, paprika, garlic powder, onion

powder, oregano, and 1/4 teaspoon kosher salt and stir.

11. Then cook without stirring for about 5 minutes or until the bottom starts to get crispy.

12. Remove from the heat and stir in 1 tablespoon lime juice and green onions. (Add any remaining lime juice to the bell pepper slaw.)

13. **Serve the quinoa tacos:** Warm the tortillas, or char them by placing a tortilla on an open gas flame on medium for a few seconds per side, flipping with tongs, until slightly blackened and warm.

14. Top the tortillas with the greens, quinoa filling, bell peppers, pickled onions, sour cream (mixed with a little hot sauce if desired) and feta crumbles.
15. Serve immediately. If desired, serve with a side of Refried Black Beans.

Best Jackfruit Tacos

The best vegan tacos? In just 20 minutes jackfruit turns into a plant-based version of pulled pork carnitas. These jackfruit tacos will amaze you.

Ingredients

For the jackfruit

- 2 15-ounce cans green jackfruit in water or brine
- 1/2 cup minced yellow onion
- 3 cloves garlic
- 2 tablespoons extra virgin olive oil
- 1 to 1 1/2 tablespoons adobo sauce (from 1 can chipotle peppers in adobo)
- 2 tablespoons cocoa powder
- 2 tablespoons tomato paste
- 2 teaspoons ground cumin
- 1 teaspoon oregano
- 1/4 teaspoon kosher salt

- 1/2 cup water
- For the tacos
- 8 tortillas (or more small street-style tortillas)
- Chopped romaine
- Fresh cilantro
- Salsa Fresca or any fresh salsa
- Refried beans, to serve on the side* (canned, Homemade Refried Beans, Instant Pot refried beans or Refried Black Beans)

Instructions

1. Rinse and drain the jackfruit in a colander, pressing down to extract as much water as

possible. Run your hands through the pieces, pulling and separating them into shreds with your fingers.

2. Mince the onion. Mince the garlic.
3. Heat the olive oil in a large skillet over medium heat.
4. Add onion and garlic and fry for 3 to 4 minutes until tender and fragrant, but before the garlic browns.
5. Add the jackfruit and remaining ingredients (add 1 tablespoon of adobo sauce for a mild recipe, up to 1 1/2 or 2 tablespoons for a spicier recipe).
6. Cook for about 5 minutes on medium low heat until saucy.

7. If desired, char the tortillas by placing them on an open gas flame on medium for a few seconds per side, flipping with tongs, until they are slightly blackened and warm.
8. To serve, place the jackfruit, romaine, salsa fresca, and torn cilantro leaves in a warmed tortilla.
9. Serve immediately with refried beans.

Quinoa Vegetarian Enchiladas

These tasty vegetarian enchiladas are a major crowd pleaser! They're stuffed with satisfying quinoa and artichoke filling.

Ingredients

For the quinoa (use Instant Pot quinoa)

- 1 1/4 cups water
- 3/4 cup quinoa, rinsed
- 1/4 teaspoon kosher salt
- For the salsa verde (substitute 2 cups purchased salsa verde)

- 1 small red onion
- 1 1/2 pounds tomatillos, husked
- 2 serrano chiles, seeded for a milder sauce
- 1/2 cup water or vegetable stock
- Kosher salt
- 1 teaspoon sugar

For the enchiladas

- 3/4 cup frozen or canned artichoke hearts (about 1 cup chopped)
- 2 tablespoons extra-virgin olive oil, plus more for the baking dish
- 10 small corn tortillas
- 2 1/2 cups grated Monterrey Jack cheese

- Handful fresh cilantro leaves, plus more for topping
- 1 cup Cotija, queso fresco, or feta cheese crumbles
- Cayenne pepper for sprinkling
- 1 lime, cut into wedges
- Sour cream or Mexican crema, to serve (optional)

Instructions

Make the quinoa:

1. Bring the water, quinoa, and salt to a boil in a medium saucepan over medium-high head.

2. Reduce the heat, cover, and simmer about 17 to 20 minutes, until the water is completely absorbed (to check, pull back the quinoa with a fork).
3. Cover and allow to steam at least 5 minutes, or until serving. (Can be made up to 2 days in advance; just be sure to cool completely and store in an airtight container.)
4. Make the salsa verde **(if using purchased, skip this step):** Halve the onion crosswise. Slice one half into very thin rings for the garnish and set aside.
5. Cut the other half into wedges. Arrange the onion wedges, tomatillos, and serranos on a baking sheet and broil until the tomatillos

are soft and browned, 15 to 20 minutes, turning with tongs halfway through cooking.

6. Transfer the onion, tomatillos, and serranos with any of their liquid to a blender or food processor, add the stock, and puree until smooth, about 3 minutes.

7. Add 1/2 teaspoon kosher salt and the sugar and pulse a few times to combine.

Make the filling:

8. Meanwhile, chop the artichoke hearts, then toss them with 2 tablespoons olive oil in a bowl and season lightly with kosher salt.

Assemble the enchiladas:

9. Steam or warm the tortillas in a microwave; keep them wrapped.
10. Toss the artichokes and quinoa with 2 cups of the Monterrey Jack cheese in a bowl.
11. Place a tortilla on the work surface. Spoon 2 to 3 tablespoons of the artichoke mixture down the middle of the enchilada, seam-side down, into the prepared baking dish.
12. Repeat with the remaining tortillas and artichoke filling, lining up the enchiladas side by side in the baking dish.
13. **Broil:** Broil until the tortillas are crisp and golden around the edges, 3 to 4 minutes.

14. Pour most of the salsa verde over and around the sides of the enchiladas and sprinkle with the remaining Monterrey Jack on top.
15. Broil until the cheese is golden brown, 1 to 2 minutes more.
16. Remove from the oven and top with the sliced onion, Cotija / queso freso / feta crumbles, and remaining cilantro.
17. **Serve:** Divide the enchiladas among plates and sprinkle them lightly with cayenne.
18. Serve warm with lime wedges. If desired, dollop with sour cream or Mexican crema.

Black Bean Burrito

The ultimate vegan burrito! A flavor-packed plant based lunch or dinner idea, it's stuffed with Mexican rice, seasoned black beans and peppers, and avocado.

Ingredients

- 2 cups cooked Spanish Rice* or Instant Pot Spanish Rice (or 2 cups cooked rice mixed with salsa, to taste)
- 2 large portobello mushroom caps
- 1/2 medium red onion
- 1 orange bell pepper

- 2 15-ounce cans black beans, drained and rinsed
- 2 tablespoons olive oil
- 2 teaspoons cumin
- 1 teaspoon garlic powder
- 1 teaspoon onion powder
- 1 teaspoon smoked paprika
- 1 teaspoon kosher salt
- 2 tablespoons lime juice
- 1 avocado
- 4 large flour tortillas or gluten-free tortillas
- **Sauce ideas (optional):** Creamy Cilantro Sauce, Vegan Queso, Spicy Chipotle Sauce, Chipotle Cream, Spicy Mayo, Vegan Sour Cream, Cashew Cream

Instructions

1. Start the Spanish Rice (aka Mexican Rice).

2. Meanwhile, remove the stems from the mushroom caps and thinly slice them.

3. Thinly slice the red onion. Thinly slice the bell pepper.

4. In a large skillet, heat the olive oil over medium high heat. Saute the veggies for 6 to 7 minutes until tender.

5. Add the black beans (drained and rinsed), garlic powder, cumin, onion powder, paprika, kosher salt, lime juice, and 2 tablespoons water. Cook for 2 minutes until heated through and the liquid evaporates.

6. Pit the avocado. Mash it and sprinkle it with kosher salt.
7. When the rice is done, finish it with the seasonings per that recipe. Then get ready to roll!
8. Place the tortillas on individual plates. Spread 1/2 cup rice on each one, at the center.
9. Top each with about a quarter of the vegetable and bean mixture, and a quarter of the avocado.
10. Add any optional sauce if desired. Fold the tortillas in half over the filling, then tuck them around and underneath the filling, forming a tight roll.

11. Fold in each side of the burritos, then roll them up. Cut in half and serve.

Vegan Fajitas

These are the very best vegan fajitas: a plant based dinner that everyone loves! Roast the veggies on a sheet pan for quick and easy prepare.

Ingredients

For the sheet pan fajita veggies

- 1 white onion
- 2 bell peppers
- 1 head cauliflower
- 1 portobello mushroom
- 2 tablespoons olive oil
- 1 tablespoon chili powder
- 1 teaspoon cumin
- 1 teaspoon smoked paprika (or regular)
- 1 teaspoon garlic powder
- 1 teaspoon onion powder
- 1 teaspoon kosher salt

For serving

- 2 ripe avocados
- 1 lime

- 1/2 teaspoon kosher salt
- Fresh cilantro
- 8 tortillas (flour or corn)
- 1 15-ounce can vegetarian refried beans or homemade refried beans

Instructions

1. Preheat the oven to 425 degrees Fahrenheit.
2. Thinly slice the onion. Slice the bell peppers. Chop the cauliflower into small florets. Chop the mushroom into bite-sized pieces.
3. Add the veggies to a big bowl and toss them with the olive oil, chili powder, cumin,

paprika, garlic powder, onion powder, and kosher salt.

4. Line 2 baking sheets with parchment paper.
5. Add the vegetables in a single layer. Roast 15 minutes, then remove the sheets, stir the veggies, and sprinkle on another 1/2 teaspoon salt spread between the trays (1/4 teaspoon on each).
6. Stir again, then return to the oven and roast another 10 minutes until tender.
7. Meanwhile, pit the avocados. Scoop out the flesh into a bowl and mash with a fork. Add the lime juice, salt, and cilantro.
8. Heat the refried beans in a small sauce pan.

9. If desired, char the tortillas by placing them on an open gas flame on medium for a few seconds per side, flipping with tongs, until they are slightly blackened and warm.
10. To serve, place the refried beans and roasted veggies in tortillas, and top with guac-ish.

Vegetarian Tortilla Soup

This vegetarian tortilla soup is so flavorful and quick! It's an easy healthy soup recipe that doesn't take too much time to prepare.

Ingredients

For the tortilla strips

- 6 6-inch corn tortillas
- Olive oil
- Kosher salt

For the vegetarian tortilla soup

- 1 yellow onion
- 1 green bell pepper

- 4 medium garlic cloves
- 2 15-ounce cans black beans
- 2 tablespoons extra-virgin olive oil, plus more for brushing
- 2 teaspoons dried oregano
- 1 teaspoon cumin
- 1 28-ounce can crushed tomatoes
- 1½ cups frozen corn (fire roasted, if possible)
- 1 tablespoon adobo sauce (from 1 can chipotle peppers in adobo sauce)
- 1 quart (4 cups) vegetable broth
- 1 teaspoon kosher salt, plus more for sprinkling
- 4 radishes, for garnish

- 1 lime, for garnish
- 1 handful cilantro, for garnish

Instructions

1. Heat oven to 375°F.
2. **Make the tortilla strips:** Brush the tortillas lightly with olive oil on each side.
3. Using a pizza cutter, slice them in half, then into thin strips.
4. Place the strips on a baking sheet and sprinkle with kosher salt. Bake for 10 to 12 minutes until crispy and lightly browned.

5. **Prep the veggies:** Peel and dice the onion. Dice the green pepper. Peel and mince the garlic. Drain and rinse the beans.
6. **Make the soup:** In a large pot or Dutch oven, heat 2 tablespoons olive oil and fry the onion until translucent, about 5 minutes.
7. Add the green pepper and the garlic and sauté for 2 minutes.
8. Stir in the oregano and the cumin for 1 minute.
9. Add the tomatoes, beans, corn, adobo sauce, broth, and kosher salt. Bring to a boil, then simmer for 10 minutes.
10. Taste and add additional adobo sauce or kosher salt if desired.

11. **Prep the garnishes:** Slice the radishes. Slice the lime into wedges.

12. **Serve:** To serve, ladle the soup into bowls and allow to cool to warm.

13. Garnish with the tortilla strips, radishes, torn cilantro leaves, hot sauce, and plenty of lime juice.

Crispy Avocado Tacos

These crispy avocado tacos are destined to be your new favorite! With crunchy breading, they've got the vibe of a fish taco but are totally plant based.

Ingredients

For the avocado tacos

- 1 recipe Baked Avocado Fries
- 15-ounce can black beans
- 1 teaspoon adobo sauce from a can of chipotle chili peppers (optional)
- 1/2 teaspoon cumin
- 1 teaspoon chili powder

- 1/2 teaspoon kosher salt
- 1 romaine head
- 1 cup pico de gallo (storebought or homemade)
- 8 flour or corn tortillas

For the cilantro sauce*

- 6 tablespoons mayonnaise (or vegan mayo or cashew cream)
- 1 1/2 tablespoons lime juice
- 1 1/2 tablespoons chopped cilantro
- 1/4 teaspoon cumin
- 1/4 teaspoon garlic powder
- 1/8 teaspoon kosher salt

Instructions

1. Make the Baked Avocado Fries.
2. While they bake, drain and rinse the beans. Mix them with with the adobo sauce, cumin, chili powder, and salt.
3. Thinly slice the romaine.
4. Make the cilantro sauce by mixing together the mayonnaise, lime juice, cilantro, cumin, garlic powder, and salt.
5. If desired, char the tortillas by placing them on an open gas flame on medium for a few seconds per side, flipping with tongs, until they are slightly blackened and warm.

6. Assemble the tacos by topping the tortillas with romaine lettuce, beans, avocado fries, pico de gallo, and cilantro sauce.

Easy Mexican Salad

This chopped Mexican salad is the best easy side dish for tacos and enchiladas! It's topped with savory cilantro lime dressing and crunchy tortilla strips.

Ingredients

- 3 Romaine hearts (8 cups chopped)
- 2 cups baby greens, like baby kale (optional)
- 1/4 cup sliced red onions (or Pickled Red Onions)
- 1/2 cup cherry tomatoes
- 4 radishes
- 1 cup frozen corn kernels, thawed
- 1 handful roasted salted pepitas (pumpkin seeds)
- **Dressing:** Cilantro Lime Dressing, Creamy Cilantro Dressing, Lime Vinaigrette **(pick one).**

- **Add-ons:** Crispy Tortilla Strips, crumbled feta or cotija cheese, chopped avocado, black beans, or chopped cucumber

Instructions

1. Make the Crispy Tortilla Strips or make them the day before and store in a sealed container in the pantry until serving.
2. **Make the dressing:** Cilantro Lime Dressing, Creamy Cilantro Dressing, or Lime Vinaigrette.
3. **Chop the vegetables:** Chop the romaine. Thinly slice the red onion. Slice tomatoes in

half. Thinly slice the radishes. Defrost the corn.

4. Prepare any other add-on veggies as appropriate.
5. Add a sprinkle of salt on the tomatoes, radishes, and corn to lightly season them.
6. **Serve:** Place the greens on the plate and top with the vegetables (and tortilla strips, if using).
7. Top with the dressing and serve. If making in advance, refrigerate the components separately; bring the dressing to room temperature before serving.

Mexican Coleslaw

This easy Mexican coleslaw recipe is deliciously fresh and tangy, featuring cabbage, red onion, cilantro, and cumin. Perfect as a side or on tacos!

Ingredients

- 8 cups shredded cabbage (1/2 large or 1 medium head green cabbage; or do half red cabbage and half green)
- 1 cup shredded carrot (1 large or 2 medium carrots)
- 1/4 red onion
- 1/2 cup finely chopped cilantro
- 1/4 cup apple cider vinegar

- 2 tablespoons olive oil
- 1/2 teaspoon cumin seed
- 1 teaspoon ground cumin
- 1 teaspoon kosher salt
- Fresh ground pepper

Instructions

1. Thinly slice the cabbage. Shred the carrot. Thinly slice the red onion. Finely chop the cilantro.
2. In a medium bowl, mix all ingredients together.
3. Taste and add additional salt or pepper if needed.

4. Serve immediately.

Note - **Make ahead:** slice the veggies in advance and store refrigerated.

Mix together with the vinegar, olive oil, cumin seed, ground cumin, salt and pepper directly before serving.

Store leftovers refrigerated; if you find the flavor needs refreshing, add a splash of vinegar, drizzle of olive oil and pinch of kosher salt to taste.)

Quinoa Taco Meat

Amazingly flavorful taco "meat" made with quinoa, smoky seasonings, and salsa! Baked until hot and crispy. A healthy substitute for ground beef.

Ingredients

Quinoa

- 1 cup tri-color, white, or red quinoa
- 1 cup vegetable broth*
- 3/4 cup water

Seasonings

- 1/2 cup salsa (slightly chunky is best)
- 1 Tbsp nutritional yeast

- 2 tsp ground cumin
- 2 tsp ground chili powder
- 1/2 tsp garlic powder
- 1/2 tsp each sea salt and black pepper
- 1 Tbsp olive or avocado oil

Instructions

1. Heat a medium saucepan over medium heat. Once hot, add rinsed quinoa and toast for 4-5 minutes, stirring frequently.
2. Add vegetable broth and water and bring back to a boil over medium-high heat.

3. Then reduce heat to low, cover with a secure lid, and cook for 15-25 minutes, or until liquid is completely absorbed.
4. Fluff with a fork, then crack lid and let rest for 10 minutes off heat.
5. Preheat oven to 375 degrees F (190 C).
6. Add cooked quinoa to a large mixing bowl and add remaining ingredients (salsa, nutritional yeast, cumin, chili powder, garlic powder, salt, pepper, and oil).
7. Toss to combine. Then spread on a lightly greased (or parchment-lined) baking sheet.
8. Bake for 20-35 minutes, stirring/tossing once at the halfway point to ensure even baking. The quinoa is done when it's

fragrant and golden brown. Be careful not to burn!

9. Store leftovers in the refrigerator up to 4-5 days. Reheat in the microwave, in a 350 degree F (176 C) oven, or in a skillet on the stovetop.

Cream of Corn Soup

This delicate Creamy Corn Soup is impressible easy to make and is the perfect soul-warming soup. No wonder corn is the base of our gastronomy in Mexico; we use it to make sweet and savory meals, as well as desserts and drinks.

Ingredients

- 2 ½ cups corn kernels removed from the cob
- 2 Tablespoons of butter
- 1/3 cup white onion finely chopped
- 2 cloves garlic diced
- 2 cups chicken broth
- 2 cups milk
- 1 tablespoons all-purpose flour
- Salt and pepper to taste

For Serving

- 1 pepper Poblano pepper roasted, cleaned, deveined, and finely chopped
- 1/2 cup Queso Fresco cut into cubes
- Salt and pepper to taste
- 4 tbsp Mexican Cream or Heavy cream for garnish optional

Instructions

1. Pull off the cornhusks from the fresh sweet corn and remove.
2. Cut the kernels using a sharp knife; be careful to remove only the grains.

3. Melt butter in a saucepan over medium-low heat.
4. Add onion and garlic. Cook, stirring to avoid sticking to the bottom until the onion and garlic are softened but not browned, about 5 minutes.
5. Increase heat to medium-high; add the corn and the 2 cups of chicken broth, bring to a simmer.
6. Reduce heat to medium-low and gently simmer for 15 minutes, or until corn is tender.
7. Once, you cook the corn, remove about 1/2 cup of kernels with a slotted spoon and reserve for garnishing.

8. While the soup simmers, mix the tablespoons of all-purpose flour with the 2 cups of milk. Mix well to avoid any lumps.
9. Place milk and flour mixture into the blender and add the cooked corn kernels with the broth.
10. Process the soup until smooth. Return pureed soup to the saucepan and simmer over medium heat until it's hot and the soup thickens about five more minutes.
11. Stir soup to avoid sticking to the pan. It should have a thick consistency. Season with salt and pepper to taste.

Vegan Mexican Lasagna

This Vegan Mexican Lasagna is layered with soft tortillas, creamy refried beans, and veggies from your garden. It's a great meal prep recipe since it freezes well, and it's ideal for feeding a crowd.

Ingredients

- 1 Tbsp. olive oil
- 1 cup yellow onion, diced
- 3 garlic cloves, minced
- 1 tsp. paprika
- ½ Tbsp. cumin
- 1 Tbsp. chili powder
- ½ tsp. sea salt

- 1 15-oz. can of refried beans (make sure they're vegetarian)
- 1 15-oz. can of black beans, drained and rinsed
- 1 14.5-oz. can of diced tomatoes, drained (or 5 to 6 fresh tomatoes, diced)
- 1 15-oz. can of corn, drained, divided
- 1 4-oz. can diced green chiles
- ¾ cup enchilada sauce
- 4 green onions, chopped, plus more for topping
- 12 taco-sized tortillas
- 1 cup vegan cheese (optional)
- Fresh cilantro and avocado, for serving

Instructions

1. Preheat your oven to 350F degrees.
2. Heat the olive oil in a large, deep skillet over medium heat.
3. Add the onion and garlic and cook until soft and fragrant, about 5 minutes.
4. Sprinkle in the spices and cook 30 seconds more. Then add in the refried beans and stir to fully combine.
5. Add the black beans, diced tomatoes, 1 cup of the corn, diced green chiles, and the green onion to the skillet, followed by the enchilada sauce.
6. Stir to combine and remove from heat.

7. Spray a 9×13 inch glass baking dish with cooking spray or rub the bottom and sides with olive oil.
8. Place two tortillas on the bottom of the baking dish; they'll overlap in the middle just slightly.
9. Cut a third tortilla into small triangles to fill in any gaps. Don't worry, it doesn't need to be perfect!
10. Add a heaping cup of the bean mixture to the dish and spread into an even layer.
11. Repeat with another layer of tortillas followed by another cup of bean mixture. In the end, you should have four layers of

tortilla and four layers of beans (the very top layer should be the bean mixture).

12. Sprinkle with vegan cheese, if using, and cover the baking dish with foil.
13. Bake the Mexican Lasagna for 20 to 25 minutes, or until the sauce is bubbly around the edges.
14. Remove from the oven and sprinkle the remaining corn and green onion over the top.
15. Garnish with fresh cilantro and sliced avocado just before serving.

Easy Calabacitas

This vegetarian Calabacitas recipe is perfect for any stubborn carnivores out there! Loads of flavor made with healthy, fresh ingredients -- yummy!!

Ingredients

- 1.5 lbs. zucchini or squash
- 1 small onion
- 3 garlic cloves
- 1 jalapeno
- 3 plum tomatoes
- 2 cups corn kernels
- 1 teaspoon Mexican oregano
- 3/4 teaspoon salt (plus more to taste)

- freshly cracked black pepper
- Cotija cheese (optional)
- freshly chopped cilantro (optional)
- olive oil

Instructions

1. Give the tomatoes a good rinse and let them roast in a 400F oven for 20 minutes or until you need them.
2. Finely chop a small onion and get it cooking in some oil over medium heat. Let it cook until it's starting to brown, approx. 7-10 minutes.

3. Add three minced garlic cloves and cook for 30-60 seconds.
4. Take a couple spoonfuls of the onion-garlic mixture from the pan and add it to the blender, this will eventually be combined with the roasted tomatoes.
5. Give the zucchinis a good rinse and cut them up into 1/4" sized pieces, be sure to cut off the ends of the zucchinis and discard.
6. Add the chopped zucchini to the onion-garlic mixture in the pan, along with 3/4 teaspoon salt, freshly cracked black pepper, and 1 teaspoon Mexican oregano.
7. Stir well and let it saute for a couple minutes as you put the tomato mixture together.

8. Rinse the jalapeno and chop it up into quarters, discarding the stem.
9. Add the roasted tomatoes to the blender along with 1/4 of the jalapeno. (There should also be a couple spoonfuls of the onion-garlic mixture in the blender.)
10. Combine well and take a taste. Add additional slivers of the jalapeno until the heat tastes right to you.
11. Add the tomato mixture back to the saucepan and let the zucchini simmer in it for a couple more minutes or until the zucchini is tender but still a little firm, this batch cooked for a total of 7-8 minutes.

Note: If using canned corn you can add it in now as it doesn't need much time to heat up. If using fresh corn kernels you can add them in when you add the zucchini.

12. Take a final taste for seasoning. You can add another pinch of salt to this batch if needed.
13. Serve immediately with your choice of garnish. (Cotija cheese and freshly chopped cilantro are good options).
14. Store leftovers in an airtight container in the fridge where they will keep for a few days.

One Skillet Mexican Quinoa Dinner

This one skillet dinner is a tasty and simple way to enjoy the health benefits of vegetables and quinoa.

Ingredients

- 1 can Pinto Beans, drained and rinsed (15.5 oz)
- 1 can Tomatoes with chiles, do not drain (10 or 15 oz)
- 1 can Corn, drained (15 oz) (or 1 cup frozen corn)
- 1 cup Quinoa

- 1 cup Vegetable Broth (low sodium preferred)
- 1 Squirt Garlic Paste (or 1 tsp minced garlic)
- 1/2 tsp Chili Powder
- 1/2 tsp Cumin
- A pinch Red Pepper Flakes
- Chopped Fresh Cilantro

Instructions

1. Combine all ingredients (Except Cilantro) in a large skillet.
2. Bring to a boil on stovetop, and then reduce heat to medium/low so that the liquid is still bubbling just a bit.

3. Cover, and let simmer and bubble a bit like this for 15 to 25 minutes, or until the liquid is absorbed and the quinoa has "burst", stirring occasionally.
4. Remove from heat, top with the chopped fresh cilantro, and serve.

Easy Mexican Street Corn (Elotes)

Mexican Street Corn or Elotes, is corn on the cob covered in creamy mayo and topped with cilantro, lime juice, Cotija cheese and chipotle chili powder. Grilled, steamed, or boiled, it's a perfectly easy Mexican summer side dish!

Ingredients

- 4 medium ears sweet corn, husks and silk removed
- 1 tablespoon cooking oil
- 1/3 cup mayonnaise
- 1 lime, juiced
- 1/2 cup crumbled cotija cheese
- 2 teaspoons chipotle chili powder
- 1/4 cup chopped cilantro

Instructions

1. Preheat a grill to medium-high heat (about 375°F-400°F).
2. Using a brush, coat each ear of corn with oil to make sure it doesn't stick to the grill during cooking.
3. Place the corn onto the grill grates, cover and let cook for about 2-3 minutes, until the corn is cooked through and charred in some spots.
4. Turn the cobs and repeat the grilling process until all the sides are cooked and browned.
5. Remove the corn from the grill and transfer to a large plate or baking sheet. (You can

also steam or boil the corn if you don't have a grill.

6. In a small bowl, add mayonnaise and lime juice. Mix together with a spoon.

7. Using a brush or a butter knife, spread the mayonnaise mixture onto each ear of grilled corn.

8. Sprinkle each ear with 2 tablespoons of Cotija cheese, 1 tablespoon of cilantro and a pinch of chili powder.

9. Taste and season with salt if desired.

Printed in Great Britain
by Amazon